MW01504731

nurses need love too!!!

Humor for Nurses;
Jokes, cartoons, tips, trivia, and more fun than changing an old man's catheter!

By Steve Lee

Morning Dew Entertainment

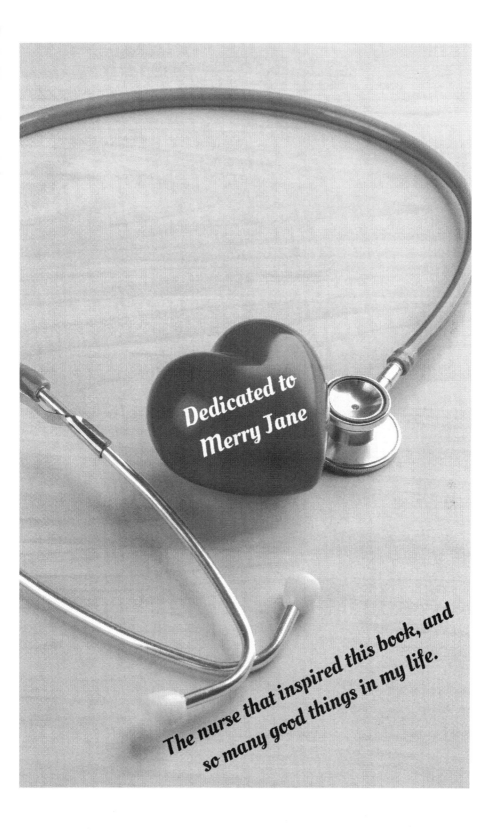

Dedicated to
Merry Jane

The nurse that inspired this book, and so many good things in my life.

TABLE OF CONTENTS

We hope you enjoy our book.
As a special gift, we are offering a FREE copy of
THE NEW SUNDAY COMICS.

FUN FACT In a poll conducted in 2001, 59 percent of nurses cited the possibility of sustaining a serious back injury as one of the top three occupational health concerns that they had.

Everyone Has A Story

When the brand new CNA in Florida showed up for her first day of work in a Senior Care Facility, she got more than she bargained for. At lunchtime, she found that all the elderly female patients were in a rush to get to the dining room.

She helped roll one the wheelchair of a particularly excited woman in her nineties down to the lunch area, only to discover that a well-proportioned male exotic dancer flaunting his wears to a cheering crowd of female patients.

The group of elderly women were stuffing money into the man's G-string faster than she thought humanly possible. Shocked and speechless, she reported the incident to the administrator. To her surprise, it turned out that this was not an isolated incident. The patients had taken a vote, and it had been unanimously agreed by staff and seniors alike that they got a "party night" once a month if everyone cooperated with the nursing staff.

The administrator concluded by saying, "This is pretty calm, you should be here for the men's "party night." It gets crazy here.

The story is true. The names, places, and a few parts have been fictionalized.

Everyone has a spirit animal to guide them.
Mine is a unicorn on a mission to poke holes in
annoying people--and you're next.

DIAGNOSIS...

Men getting catheters!!!

REALITY CHECK

WHAT A GUY
DREAMS OF
WHEN HE
THINKS
ABOUT
DATING A
NURSE...

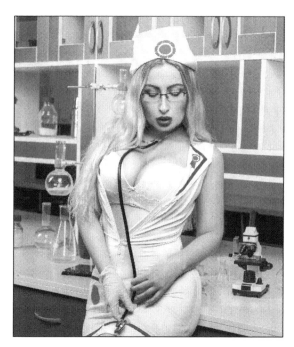

WHAT A GUY
GETS WHEN
HE'S DATING
A NURSE.

WELCOME
TO THE
REAL
WORLD!

6

GIVEN MISTER JONES'S ZERO TOLERANCE FOR PAIN, HE WAS CERTAIN THAT NURSE RACHET WAS USING A SPORTS BALL'S INFLATING NEEDLE TO GIVE HIM THE INJECTION.

Warning Bad Joke Zone

HOW DO YOU KNOW WHEN A NURSE IS HAVING A BAD DAY?

SHE WON'T STOP NEEDLING PEOPLE.

7

DID YOU KNOW?

The common symbol for a pharmacy is represented by a bowl and a snake. But who's bowl is represented in this symbol?

The Bowl of Hygieia is one of the two main symbols of pharmacology. Along with the Rod of Asclepius, it is one of the oldest and most important western medical symbols. Hygieia was the Greek goddess of health and cleanliness. She was either Asclepius's partner, wife, or daughter. Asclepius's symbol is his staff with a snake wrapped around it. Hygieia's symbol is a cup or chalice with a snake wrapped around the stem and sitting on top of it.

Time & PERSPECTIVE

GRADE SCHOOL

Oh no, I missed the answer.

VERSUS

Yes!!! I got the answer

NURSING SCHOOL

REST IN PEACE

If I'm going to go crazy,
I'd rather drive myself.

THE NURSING DREAM

Just because someone has changed the staffing ratios, doesn't mean that you are adequately staffed.

Everyone Has A Story

A man in Eastern Canada was brought into the E.R. after drinking too much out on his boat.

The man had docked his boat, climbed out, and stumbled up the dock to the boat shed at which point the alcohol and his wobbly sea legs got the best of him.

As he began to topple over, he grabbed a large tool chest to keep from falling, but instead had pulled the heavy chest over on top of him. He hit his head on a nearby boat trailer on the way down. Hours later the man was found still out cold by a local fisherman who called the authorities.

The man woke up in the E.R. only to find that the tool chest had landed in such a way that it cut off circulation to his most personal tool. Without circulation for several hours, the man had to have the little guy removed.

That was the worst day of his life.

OUCH!

The story is true. The names, places, and a few parts have been fictionalized.

13

"As a nurse, we have the opportunity to heal the heart, mind, soul, and body of our patients, their families and ourselves. They may forget your name, but they will never forget how you made them feel."
                                        – Maya Angelou

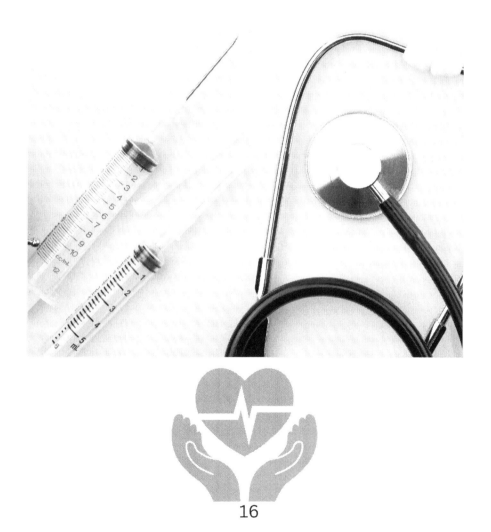

IF YOUR BIKE IS ON FIRE...

AND YOU ARE ON FIRE...

ON A BIKE WITH SQUARE TIRES...

GOING UPHILL IN HELL!!!

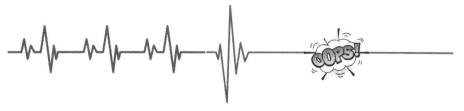

Nursing School 101

Rule 3: Caffeine is its own distinct category of food group. You will understand this better after your first week on the job.

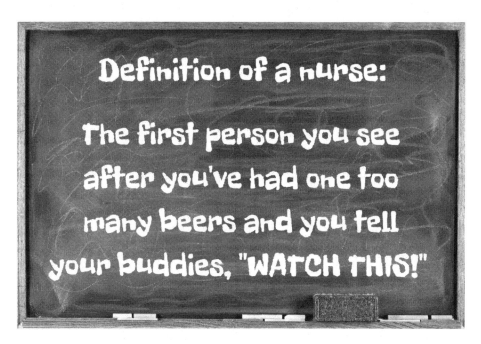

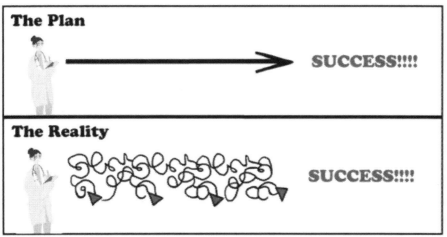

CH...CH...CHANGES!

INTRODUCING OUR NIGHT SHIFT

ON-CALL SURGEON: VERY EXPERIENCED

AFTER HOURS OPERATIONS MANAGER: ALWAYS WRAPPED UP IN HIS OWN ISSUES.

RADIOLOGIST: NOBODY CAN READ X-RAYS LIKE THIS GUY

FIRST-YEAR INTERN: HE'S YOUNG, BUT ENTHUSIASTIC!

CNA: SHE'S NICE, KEEPS TO HERSELF.

HEAD FLOOR NURSE: SHE'S GREAT, JUST DON'T PISS HER OFF.

LAB TECH: YOU'LL LOVE THIS GUY.

LPN: SUCH A DRAMA QUEEN!

THE NEW GUY: WE DON'T KNOW MUCH ABOUT HIM---

23

YOUR LIFE, YOUR CHOICE!!

Foley catheters for Women

Is the Foley catheter not quite on target? Try this tip to make your life a little easier.

Not just inexperienced nurses frequently miss the mark. Whether you are a veteran or not, the fact is that we have all got our fair share of experience. If you attempt to insert a Foley catheter into a female patient and are unsuccessful in getting a return, leave the first catheter in place and repeat the treatment with a second Foley catheter, this time aiming higher.

Me when a patient is noncompliant!

Our home health and hospice agency is looking for an angel investor.

DR. JOHNSON COULD NEVER UNDERSTAND WHY THE NURSING STAFF SAID THAT HE NEEDED TO IMPROVE HIS BEDSIDE MANNER.

Nursing School 101

Rule 21: You cannot fix crazy. You just have to document it.

DAY IN THE LIFE OF A CASE MANAGER

FINALLY, MY DESK IS CLEAN.

Everyone Has A Story

A young adult who had been prescribed a patch that included amphetamine and dextroamphetamine salts came in for his two-week follow-up appointment. The patient said that he was having problems with the new medication. He told the nurse that the doctor had told him to put a new patch on daily.

The nurse asked if he was having side effects, and he said no, but that he was running out of places to put them. He then pulled off his t-shirt to reveal fourteen patches all over his upper arms and chest.

"You do realize that you are supposed to remove the old patch before applying the new one." The nurse said as she showed him the instructions included with the prescription.

"It doesn't have pictures." The young man said. "I have ADHD, so I don't read. I only look at pictures."

The story is true. The names, places, and a few parts have been fictionalized.

WHAT?

If you don't get this, you've never dealt with CoPs.

"We have all kinds of Regulatory Guidelines floating around."

Being a nurse is easy,
It the jerks that are hard

DID YOU KNOW?

Nursing is as old as the history of mankind. Old Latin texts from the fifth century contain the word nutricius, which meant "to nourish or nourishing." Middle English texts from the thirteenth century use the word nurice, and old French texts from the eighteenth century use the word nourice. All three forms of the word nurse mean the same thing.

HEALTHY FOR TODAY AND TOMORROW

Nursing School 101

Rule 32: You do not determine the difference between an oral and a rectal thermometer by taste.

I'M NOT CRAZY, I PREFER TO BE CONSIDERED PSYCHOLOGICALLY INTOXICATED!

I know this sounds a little kooky, but what if we actually listened to our medical staff's suggestions? . . . No, now that I think about it, that's just crazy.

Before you hire someone, put them in front of a computer with slow internet, then decide.

NURSE GRUMPY

DID YOU KNOW?

The history of the male nurse and nursing have frequently been seen as being interchangeable. Contrary to popular belief, males have always had a leading role in what we now refer to as nursing care dating back to before the time of Christ. Women have only risen to prominence in nursing over the past 166 years, accounting for approximately 90% of the profession's current workforce worldwide.

"It is not how much we do — it is how much love we put into the doing."

– Mother Teresa

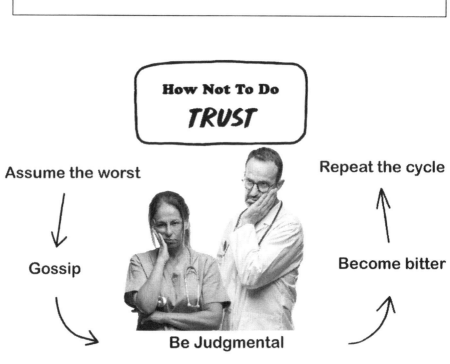

Nursing School 101

Rule 13: When dealing with a "code brown," consider using the triple glove option. It really works.

YOU KNOW THAT DIRTY OLD MAN IN ROOM 209 THAT'S ALWAYS TRYING TO GRAB MY ASS. HE NEARLY DIED TODAY...BUT THEN I TOOK A DEEP BREATH, COUNTED TO TEN, AND PUT THE SCALPEL AWAY. HE DIDN'T HAVE A CLUE.

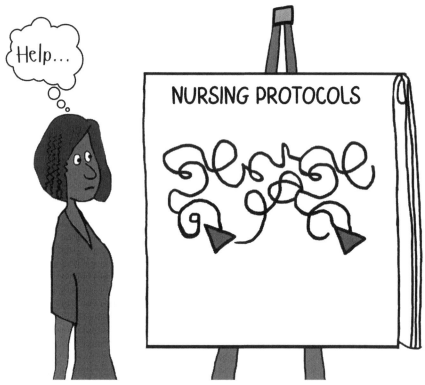

7 Essential Tips For New Nurses

- Never Be Afraid to Ask Questions, even if you think they are dumb or irrelevant.
- Always make sure that your patients are your top priority.
- Lean on, and learn from experienced nurses.
- Make real friendships with your coworkers. It will get you through the hard times and make the easy times more fun.
- Always, always, always be willing to learn, and then keep learning.
- Remember that a nurse's career path isn't linear. There are many paths a nurse can take. If you don't like your current trajectory, there are plenty of options available to you.

"I'd like you to work more than just 24/7."

Bitch Please...

ONLY NURSES AND UNICORNS CAN
FART RAINBOWS!

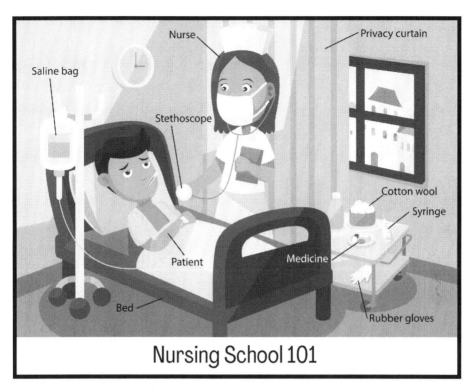

Nursing School 101

"I don't think he's sleeping, I think he's faking."

Nursing School 101

Rule 102: It is a good idea to always keep a spare set of scrubs in your locker. If you don't understand why -- you will.

How to avoid throwing up in unpleasant circumstances.

For smelly conditions, use peppermint oil in your mask. Put a few drops of peppermint oil in your face mask and breathe through your mouth.

This is also beneficial for patients who feel like vomiting due to unpleasant smells.

Plan B: Consider wearing two masks. Spread a little toothpaste (or peppermint oil) inside the second one. This makes it easier for you to bear the smell and prevents toothpaste or peppermint oil from getting on your face or beard.

I ADHERE TO THE WISDOM OF MAE WEST, WHO SAID...

When choosing between two evils,

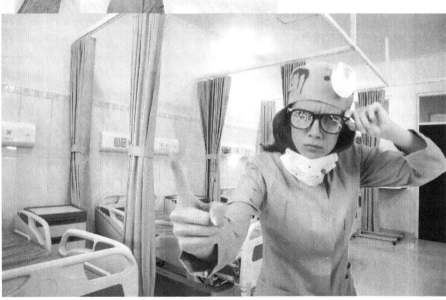

I always pick the one I've never tried before.

"You're allergic to feathers."

DR. GLASS HALF FULL

48

Everyone Has a Story

When a mother from Upstate New York took her infant child to her pediatrician, stating that her baby was rubbing her ears and crying.

After a brief exam, it was quickly established that the child was suffering from an earache. Eardrops were prescribed for the child. The Doctor wrote the prescription, "Put two drops in the right ear every four hours." The pediatrician abbreviated "right" as an R with a circle around it.
After a few days had passed, the mother came back with her child and complained that the child still had an earache and that the baby's rear end was growing quite greasy from all of the drips of oil that had been applied.

When the doctor looked at the bottle of eardrops and then discovered the problem as he read the label. The pharmacist had the following instructions typed on the label: "Put two drops in R ear every four hours."

Problem solved.

YOU'VE GOT TO ADMIT, YOU'VE THOUGHT ABOUT DOING THIS AT LEAST ONCE...

"You are perfectly sound."

"Team development needs work.
how about if we go to a training seminar ...
just to get out of the woods?"

Most days I love my job.

But there are those days...

When I would love a job where I can push terrified skydiving students out of a plane!

"The yellow stain on his chest?
My theory is too much mustard."

"Teachers and nurses get the best seats in Heaven."

— *Arnold Schwarzenegger*

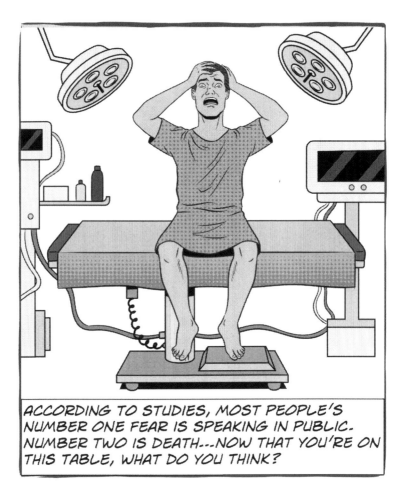

ACCORDING TO STUDIES, MOST PEOPLE'S NUMBER ONE FEAR IS SPEAKING IN PUBLIC. NUMBER TWO IS DEATH...NOW THAT YOU'RE ON THIS TABLE, WHAT DO YOU THINK?

INTERESTING FACTS

The nurse's cap, which is designed to keep one's hair in order, is fashioned after the habit worn by nuns. In spite of the fact that it has been known for some time that this article of clothing harbors infectious agents, some nations continue to have their female nurses wear it as part of their uniform.

IT DOESN'T MATTER WHAT YOU READ ON THE INTERNET, IT IS NOT AN ALIEN.

Hey mom and dad, I'm home, I'm broke, and I'm willing to discuss going to medical school.

Nursing School 101

Rule 29: For a patient's easier evacuation from a bedpan, powder it before placing them on it; this is especially helpful for overweight patients.

Why does everyone always think the internet has the right answers and consider it as a second opinion?

Change is inevitable-- except in the breakroom's vending machine

DID YOU KNOW?

According to a report that was published in 1996 by the National Institute of Occupational Safety and Health (NIOSH), one million workers are assaulted on the job each and every year, and the majority of these assaults occur in service settings such as hospitals, nursing homes, and social service agencies.

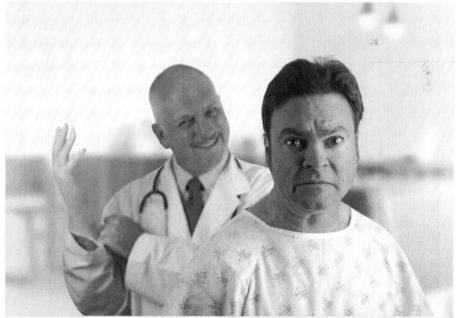

NOW COMES THE WORST PART OF THE EXAM. AFTER I FINISH YOUR PROSTATE EXAM, I'LL BE RUNNING YOUR CREDIT CARD.

"The hospital computer system has a virus. Ironic, isn't it?"

"I know my instruments are sterilized every day
but I have no idea who does it."

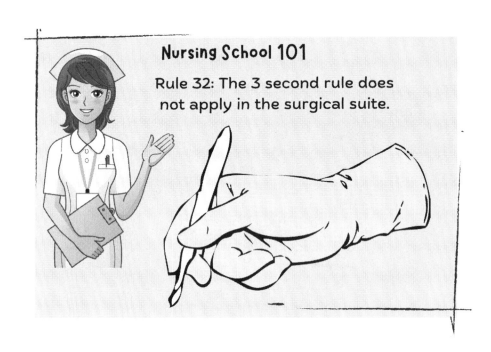

Rule #1: The nurse is always right.
Rule #2: If you think she is wrong, then slap yourself and refer back to rule #1

Everyone Has a Story

A mother in the deep South rushed her infant into the ER because the child was shaking and had an extreme heart rate. The staff immediately started running tests on the child as they asked the mother a series of questions about the child. The mother explained that she had simply given her baby formula, and the baby had started shaking. They asked what brand of formula. It was a well-known and reliable brand, so the question was asked if the family had any allergies. The mom shook her head and told them that she wasn't aware of anything.

Perplexed, they continued to question the mom, but nothing seemed to click until the mother mentioned that she drank high-caffeine energy drinks.

Then came the shocking revelation that the mother had mixed the formula with the energy drink. After getting the baby's heartbeat back under control, the Doctor explained to the mother that energy drinks can never be given to babies. The mother smiled and said, "Then maybe he will sleep through the night now."

Ya Think?

The story is true. The names, places, and a few parts have been fictionalized.

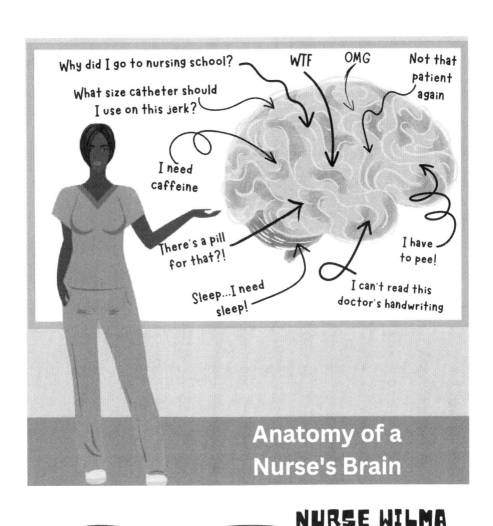

DAY iN THE LiFE OF A CASE MANAGER

Doctors: The 3 Stages of Liability Insurance

"It sounds angry. We can come back tomorrow
and ask about our benefits."

Nursing School 101

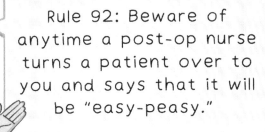

Rule 92: Beware of anytime a post-op nurse turns a patient over to you and says that it will be "easy-peasy."

I CAN EXPLAIN IT TO YOU AGAIN, BUT THERE'S NO WAY ON GOD'S GREEN EARTH THAT I CAN UNDERSTAND IT FOR YOU.

BUT I DON'T GET IT?

I don't know why people say nursing is stressful. I just had my 35th birthday, and I feel great.

Me, when I hear my patient tell the doctor, "my nurse never told me that" - -just after I had told him that.

To be clear, I DO NOT curse like a sailor. I do, however, cuss like a nurse who has had 2 code browns, no lunch, no pee break, and a F*#k@#! survey all in one shift.

HOW DOCTORS THINK THEIR NURSING STAFF ALWAYS FEEL ABOUT THEM.

Put the cane down, or the next catheter I use will be a 24.

The paperwork crept closer and closer.

"See that dark spot? That's potential litigation."

75

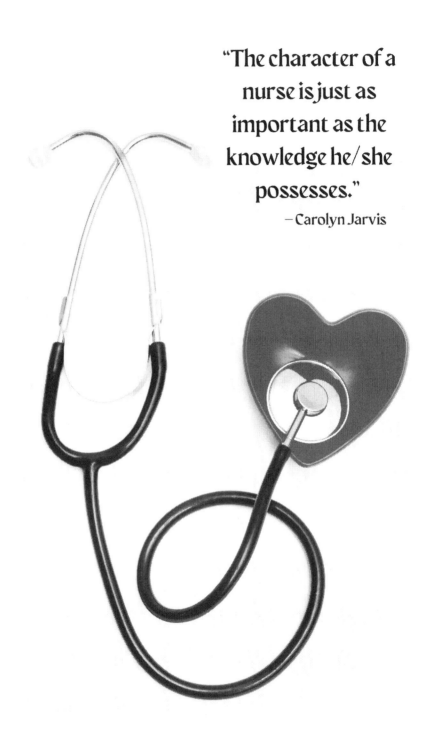

"The character of a
nurse is just as
important as the
knowledge he/she
possesses."

– Carolyn Jarvis

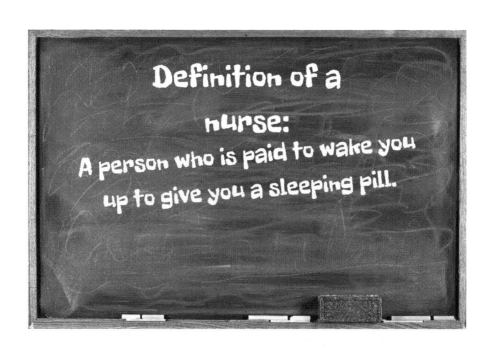

The day you understand
why a pizza is made round,
packaged in a square box,
and sliced into triangles;
then you will begin to
understand nurses.

DO YOU REALLY WANT TO PUSH THAT CALL
BUTTON AGAIN???

Everyone Has A Story

After graduating from Nursing School, I took a job in southern Arizona. My first patient was a Mexican in both renal failure and liver failure. He only spoke French, and I only knew about ten words in Spanish, which wasn't much help.

The man had numerous tattoos and appeared to have been in some sort of gang in his youth. Pushing fifty, this guy was just a scared, confused person who was afraid to die. The floor nurse said that they were short-staffed and that I would have to manage him by myself. It was then that I learned that he had an open wound on his penis. My job included cleaning him and applying antibiotic ointment to the wound twice a day. Most of my day was spent pleading with him to stop touching his penis by using hand gestures and drawings because he was so confused and just knew it hurt there. After eight hours of this back and forth, the man grabbed one of my breasts and squeezed until I yelped in pain.

"Duele, duele!" he cried out.

I later found out that meant "it hurts" in Spanish. As I looked at the bruises on my chest, I had to agree; and I never went back into the man's room again.

Nursing School Has Been Proven to Age You

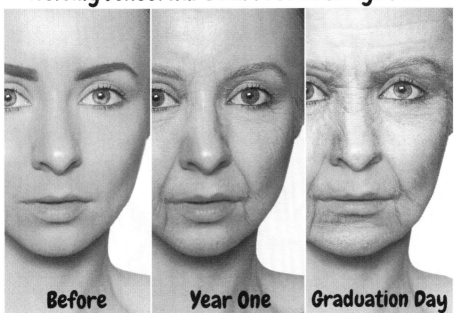

Before   Year One   Graduation Day

YES, MY BLOOD TYPE IS COFFEE. DO YOU HAVE A PROBLEM WITH THAT?

You know that you're a real nurse when you baste your turkey with a piston syringe.

Life at nursing school

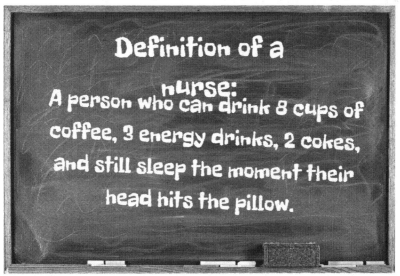

83

Me trying to tell the perky new day-shift nurse what happened during the night shift.

Today's to do list.

✦

"The operation was a success, and after another
week or so of pleading, I'm confident
that I'll convince the HMO to pay for it."

85

Nursing School 101

Rule 47: Keep the following in order:
1st- Coffee before your shift.
2nd- Alcohol after the sh*t--I mean shift.

"Can I buy a vowel, Pat?"

I KNOW THAT YOU WANT TO BE SICK, DEAR.
BUT MOMMY IS A NURSE. SO YES, YOU
HAVE TO GO TO SCHOOL.

I understand that you are hungry, but you're still NPO. And just so you know, I haven't eaten anything for the last twelve hours either, nor have I been lying in bed.

"You're reached the wrong department.
Let me transfer you to a place
called Nowhere."

Everyone Has A Story

A man in northern Massachusetts was brought into the ER for multiple injuries. When the attending doctor asked what had happened, it became so painfully funny that he had to leave the room.

The man's wife had been attempting to apply hairspray, but the spray tip had clogged. She used a safety pin to clear the opening and then sprayed a liberal amount of the spray into the toilet. Once she got the clog cleared, she finished her hair and left the bathroom.

Her husband came in a little while later to do his business. He sat on the toilet and lit up a smoke. As he had done hundreds of times before, he then dropped the still-burning match between his legs to extinguish it.

However, this time the match did not extinguish, it created a fireball under the man's butt. Surprised by the fiery explosion, the man jumped up (his pants still at his ankles) and ended up faceplanting into the bathroom closet across the tiny bathroom, knocking him unconscious.

His wife came running back after hearing her husband shriek followed by a smack and ending with a dull thud. She found him unconscious on the floor with his bare butt facing skyward.

She immediately called 911. Minutes later the ambulance and police arrived. The wife was explaining the entire story to the officers while the paramedics were taking her husband out on a gurney. The paramedics started laughing so hard as they were going down the stairs that they tipped the gurney just enough to drop the man. He hit the stair edge with such force that he fractured his hip.

And this was his condition when he arrived at the E.R. Now you know why the attending doctor had to leave the room to gain his composure.

The story is true. The names, places, and a few parts have been fictionalized.

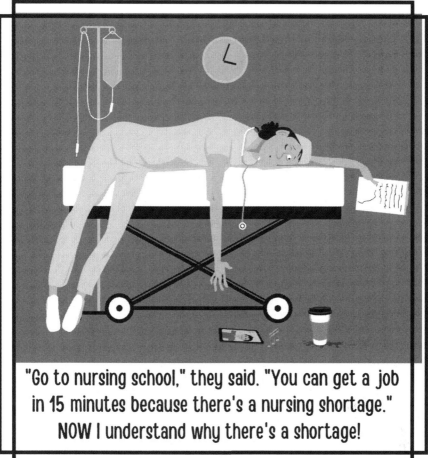

"Go to nursing school," they said. "You can get a job in 15 minutes because there's a nursing shortage." NOW I understand why there's a shortage!

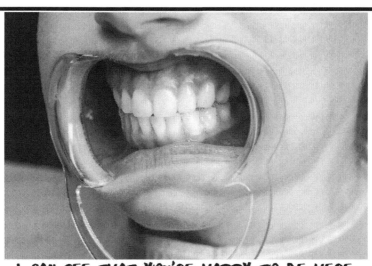

I CAN SEE THAT YOU'RE HAPPY TO BE HERE.

IN NURSING SCHOOL, THEY TAUGHT ME TO EXPECT THE UNEXPECTED...

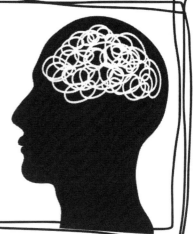

At the end of the shift, trying to remember a patient's name just after they gave it to me.

"Save one life, and you're a hero. Save a hundred lives, and you're a nurse."

—Unknown

HOW TO TELL WHEN A NURSING STUDENT IS GOOD TO GO.

A recent study found that the average nurse walks around 875 miles a year, and another study found that nurses drink an average of 38 gallons of coffee per year. Which means on average, nurses get around 23 miles to the gallon.   Guess there are no hybrids here.

I went to 6 years of school to become a nurse anesthetist. Why do you ask?

Life as an ER nurse is when the dark circles under your eyes are bigger than your circle of friends.

AFTER A 12-HOUR SHIFT AND THE D.O.N. TELLS ME THAT THEY NEED ME TO PULL A DOUBLE.

DO I HAVE TO SPELL IT OUT FOR YOU

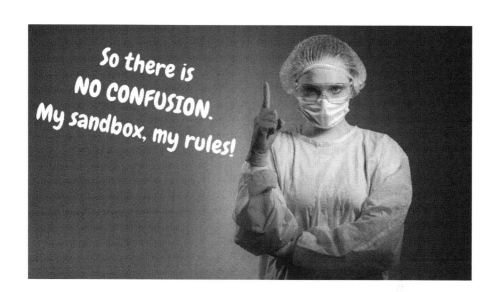

"You think you have it rough.
Try organizing a waiting room."

Nursing School 101

Rule 44: Anything that makes your brain go into overload means something is most likely wrong. Stop tinkering and get a second opinion.

WANTED

MY MIND BACK

At the moment, I am unsupervised. And yes, it freaks me out too... but damn, the possibilities are endless.

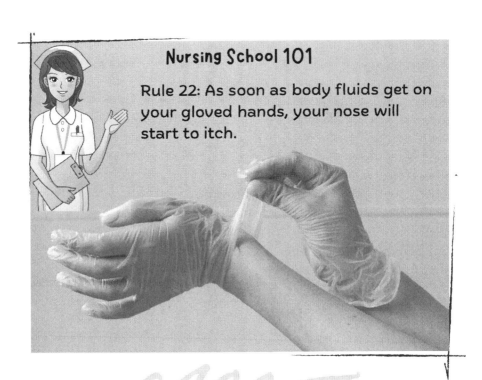

Nursing School 101

Rule 22: As soon as body fluids get on your gloved hands, your nose will start to itch.

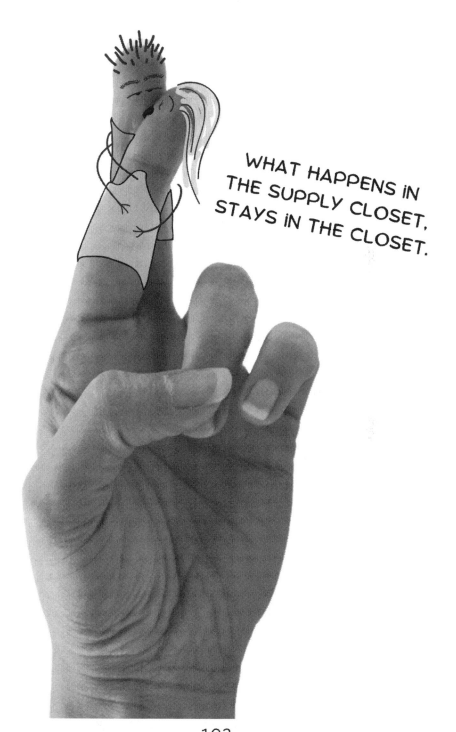

WHAT HAPPENS IN
THE SUPPLY CLOSET,
STAYS IN THE CLOSET.

What do you call a student in nursing school who only got Cs?

Hopefully not a nurse!

My goal is to remain calm
when everything is falling apart.

DID YOU KNOW?

The Lily-Of-The-Valley as medicine?

In some parts of the world, the root, underground stem (rhizome), and dried flower tips of the Lily-of-the-Valley plant are used to make medicine. They are used to treat issues with the heart, like heart failure and an irregular heartbeat. But the Lily-of-the-Valley is also very dangerous if you don't know how to use it. Lily of the valley can kill, especially children, if they eat the flowers or even drink water from a vase that the flowers have been stored in.

❖

What happens when a nurse gets strep throat on Friday afternoon?

They end up with Saturday Night Fever!

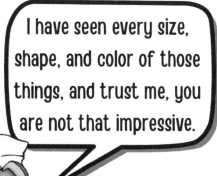

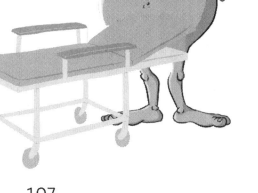

The average nursing school ratio: women to men 15 to 1

Every once in a while, there is the perfect day!

This book is written in appreciation for all the great medical professionals that put their hearts and souls out there every day for the rest of us.

Thanks

ONE LAST NOTE:

If you liked this book, we would really appreciate it if you could leave us a review. Your reviews make us as happy as a hot cup of coffee and an hour with no-call lights.

Smilin'
Steve

SMILIN' STEVE LEE LOVES HAVING FUN. HIS MOTTO IS "FUNNY FIRST."
FOR THE LAST 22 YEARS (& STILL GOING STRONG), HE HAS BEEN
MARRIED TO ONE OF THE SWEETEST, COOLEST, AND MOST FUN NURSES
ON THE PLANET.

STEVE'S NUMBER ONE GOAL IN BRINGING YOU THIS BOOK IS TO ADD A
LITTLE LAUGHTER TO YOUR LIFE.   HOPEFULLY, YOU'VE HAD SOME FUN
READING IT.

We hope that you have enjoyed our book.

As a special gift, we are offering a FREE copy of
THE NEW SUNDAY COMICS.

Or visit us here:

ILoveGoodBooks.net/freestuff

IF YOU ENJOYED THIS BOOK, AND YOU LOVE FISHING, CHECK THIS OUT;

References

CHCM. (2022, August 10). Nurse Facts. Creative Heath Care Management. https://chcm.com/nurse-facts/

Editorial Team. (2022, June 16). 14 Most Interesting Facts About Nursing. EveryNurse.org. https://everynurse.org/14-interesting-facts-nursing/

Hammer, R. (2021, March 18). 10 Funny Healthcare Doctor Stories (For your Laughing Pleasure). ReferralMD. https://getreferralmd.com/2013/09/10-funny-healthcare-stories-memes-laughing-pleasure/

Kleber, M. K. R. N. (2021, March 18). 35+ Nurse Hacks That Will Save Your Sanity. FreshRN. https://www.freshrn.com/nurse-hacks/

Mir, A. (2021, March 8). Nursing Tips & Tricks: Essential Nursing Hacks. Medical-Locums Group. https://www.medical-locums.co.uk/news/2020/08/nursing-tips-tricks-essential-nursing-hacks

Monika. (2022, October 4). Doctors Are Sharing Their Stupidest And Funniest Patient Stories, And It's Hilarious. Bored Panda. https://www.boredpanda.com/funny-doctor-patient-stories/?utm_source=google

Norris, R. C. N. (2022, September 23). Nurse Hacks for the Happy Nurse. Incredible Health. https://www.incrediblehealth.com/blog/nurse-hacks-for-the-happy-nurse/

Nursing Career Facts. (n.d.). Retrieved October 26, 2022, from https://www.aacnnursing.org/Students/Your-Nursing-Career-A-Look-at-the-Facts

Team, T. N. B. (2022, October 26). Funny, Shocking And Silly Nursing Stories - A LIVE FEED. The Nurse Break. https://thenursebreak.org/breakroom-funny-stories/

Whelan, C. (n.d.). 8 Funny (& Very, Very Real) Nursing Stories. Retrieved October 26, 2022, from https://www.berxi.com/resources/articles/real-and-funny-nursing-stories/

Writers, S. (2022, October 24). Tips For Nurses In Their First Year. NurseJournal. https://nursejournal.org/articles/tips-for-nurses-in-their-first-year/

Special thanks for the additional photography & vectors provided by 123rf.com, depositphotos.com, vecteezy.com; in accordance with their standard licensing agreements.

Please check out all our books at

ILoveGoodBooks.net

Made in the USA
Las Vegas, NV
06 November 2023

80341877R00068